W9-AUQ-438

ARIZONA

Copyright © 1986 Raintree Publishers Limited Partnership

A Turner Educational Services, Inc. book. Based on the Portrait
of America television series created by R.E. (Ted) Turner.

Library of Congress Number: 85-9978

45678910   949392919089

Library of Congress Cataloging in Publication Data

Thompson, Kathleen.
   Arizona.

   (Portrait of America)
   "A Turner book."
   Summary: Discusses the history, economy, culture,
and future of Arizona. Also includes a state
chronology, pertinent statistics, and maps.
   1. Arizona—Juvenile literature. [1. Arizona]
I. Title. II. Series: Thompson, Kathleen. Portrait of
America.
F811.3.T46   1985   979.1   85-9978
ISBN 0-86514-425-7 (lib. bdg.)
ISBN 0-86514-500-8 (softcover)

Cover Photo: United States Department of the Interior

★ ★ ★ ★ ★
Portrait of AMERICA

ARIZONA

Kathleen Thompson

A TURNER BOOK
RAINTREE PUBLISHERS

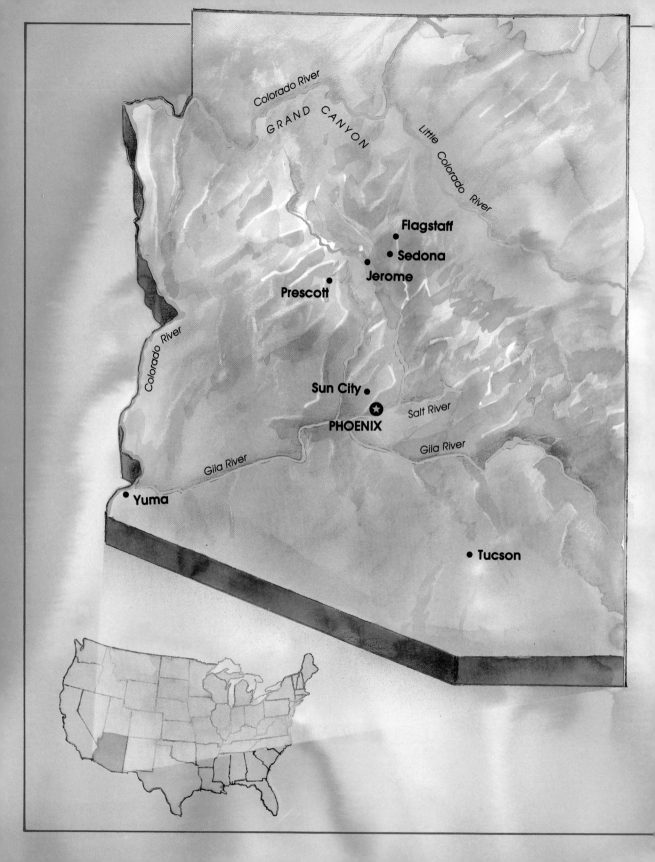

CONTENTS

Introduction

Arizona, the Grand Canyon State.

"I'm continually impressed with the place. It's just an overpowering place. The age of the rocks! These rocks that we're sitting on are over a billion and a half years old! . . . Of course, the normal reaction is to say that life is pretty insignificant, given that expanse of time. But really, it is quite precious."

Arizona: desert, adobe, and high tech.

"Well, I'm twenty-five and I graduated from Purdue University in Indiana. Primarily from the Midwest. My background is engineering and the so-called high-tech industries are here in Phoenix. The future that I have in mind for myself and my family is more attainable here."

Arizona is a dramatically beautiful land of deserts and canyons and rugged mountains. It is dry. That may be the single most important fact about the state. There is very little water here.

But on this dry land, technology is busily creating a Garden of Eden. Because of its beauty and its amazing climate, people want to live in Arizona and they are using modern technology to make that possible.

The question is, will modern Americans succeed where ancient cultures failed? Do we have enough respect for the land to tame it without destroying it?

The Old History and the New History

In Egyptian mythology, the phoenix was a bird that lived for five hundred years and then burst into flame. When the fire died, the phoenix was born again from its own ashes.

The myth of the phoenix is a good one to keep in mind while looking at the history of Arizona. Much of the area is desert. And on this desert, civilizations come and go like the phoenix.

Three centuries before Jesus was born in Nazareth, the Hohokam Indians lived on the land of Arizona. They irrigated the desert with long, deep irrigation ditches and made it bloom, much as it does today. Their civilization was sophisticated. Archaeologists believe they have found an

More than 200 Hohokam Indians lived in Montezuma Castle (left) over 800 years ago.

Salt River Project

© Patrick Dean

Hohokam Indians (shown in the painting above) lived in Arizona more than 2,000 years ago. The figures on the rock (below, left) were made by the Hohokam. The Arizona desert (left) looks much the same today as it did when the Hohokam were in Arizona.

observatory used by the Hohokam to chart the courses of the stars.

The Hohokam civilization lasted for over a thousand years. That's five times as long as the United States has been a country. Compared to that old history in Arizona, the new history has barely begun.

But, suddenly, the Hohokam disappeared. No one knows what happened. It could have been weather or war. There's no way to tell. But the name Hohokam means "those who left."

And the desert took back the land. The vast fields of the Hohokam returned to the cactus and the lizards. But the descendants of the Hohokam, the Papago and the Pima Indians, began again.

In the northern part of Arizona, the Anasazi Indians, ancestors of the Pueblo Indians, also created a culture. In Arizona and in nearby New Mexico they built stone apartment buildings with hundreds of rooms. They were as expert in using different kinds of stone as we are in using different kinds of metal.

The Anasazi, too, disappeared. Their civilization, too, returned to sand and stone.

When the Navajo and Apache Indians came into Arizona, only a few hundred years ago, they found the Papago and the Pima, the Pueblo and the Mogollon.

The Hopi village in what is now Navajo County is the oldest continuously inhabited community in the United States. In Arizona, the phoenix is always reborn.

In the early 1500s, the first Europeans began to come to Arizona. They began the new history.

The new history started with stories of gold. When Spanish explorers came to this continent, they were looking for riches to take back to their own country. To them, as to other European explorers, this new world was little more than a treasure hunt.

When stories began to reach Mexico of seven golden cities to the north, explorers came in search of them. The first European to enter Arizona was Marcos de Niza. He was a Franciscan priest and he was looking for the seven cities. He passed through Arizona in 1539.

Of course, Marcos didn't find the seven cities. But, for some reason, when he went back to Mexico he claimed that he had seen them. He described them in such glittering detail that, the next year, the famous explorer Coronado headed north to continue the search. He, too, passed through Arizona.

It wasn't until more than a

hundred years later that Europeans first came to Arizona to stay. In 1692, Father Eusebio Kino, a Jesuit priest, came into the area. He established twenty-four missions and explored much of the state.

The missions in Arizona were not simply churches. The priests of the missions were representatives of the Spanish government. It was their job to convert the Indians to Christianity, but also to the Spanish culture. They taught the Indians of the area the Spanish language. In many cases, the age-old culture of a tribe was lost and replaced by the foreign ways of the priests.

Many Indians in Arizona resisted the Spanish. But the heavily armed Spanish soldiers usually won. In 1752, the first European settlement was founded at Tubac. It was a fort built by the soldiers.

In 1776, the same year that the thirteen colonies on the east coast declared their indepen-dence from Great Britain, Tucson became a Spanish fort. Inside the fort, soldiers lived with their families. Outside, the Apaches became fiercer in their attempt to save their homes.

To the south, the people of Mexico were fighting to gain their independence from Spain. In 1821, they won. All of the area in the Southwest that had been claimed by the Spanish was

On the right-hand page is the San Xavier del Bac mission, near Tucson. The building was built about 200 years ago, but the mission was first founded in 1700 by Father Eusebio Kino (right).

Arizona Historical Society Museum

now considered part of Mexico.

But by this time, American and French frontiersmen had begun to come into the area. In parts of what is now the American Southwest there were now large U.S. settlements. And the people in these areas wanted to be free of Mexico.

In 1846, Mexico and the United States went to war. When the war ended in 1848, Mexico agreed to a treaty that gave the United States the area called New Mexico. That area included most of Arizona. In 1853, the Gadsden Purchase gave the United States the rest of Arizona.

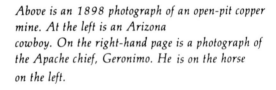

Above is an 1898 photograph of an open-pit copper mine. At the left is an Arizona cowboy. On the right-hand page is a photograph of the Apache chief, Geronimo. He is on the horse on the left.

There were a lot of people in the country who didn't think the government had made a very good deal. The land, after all, was just desert, not good for much of anything.

But settlers came to Arizona. It was rough country, the land of the cowboy and the outlaw. It was the West.

In 1850, Arizona settlers asked Congress to create an Arizona territory. Their request was refused. Then, in 1861, the Civil War began. Many of the settlers in the area were from the South. They wanted to be part of the

Confederacy. And in 1863, the Confederacy granted them what the U.S. Congress had refused. It declared that Arizona was now the Confederate Territory of Arizona.

As it happens, this didn't mean much. When Confederate troops tried to gain control of the area, they were soundly defeated by Union troops. But the action of the Confederacy lit a fire under the U.S. Congress, and in 1863, they created the Arizona Territory.

This period of history in Arizona is what we see—filtered through someone's imagination—in all those old cowboy movies. Kit Carson came out and fought the Navajos. The Apaches, led by Cochise and Geronimo, mounted horses, which had been brought to the country years ago by the Spanish, and raided farms that were built on their land. Wyatt Earp and the Clanton brothers shot each other up in the O.K. Corral. Zane Grey wrote about it all in books like *Riders of the Purple Sage.*

Miners came in looking, like Coronado, for wealth beyond their wildest dreams. When they didn't find it, they left behind towns called Ft. Misery, Lousy Gulch, and Total Wreck. When they did find wealth, in the copper mines of the 1870s and 1880s, they built boom towns that were as wild as any the cowboys had ever known.

Farmers began irrigating their fields. Ranching became big business. And in 1877, the railroad came through from California.

The people of Arizona decided it was time that they became a state. But once again, Congress didn't cooperate. Finally, in 1905, bills were presented in Congress that would have made one large state out of the Arizona and New Mexico territories. But the voters in Arizona said no.

In 1910, Arizona applied for statehood by itself, with a constitution of its own. President Taft said no. It seems that the constitution had a clause in it that would allow Arizona voters to remove their judges from office by a process called recall. Taft said that this was unacceptable, so the people of Arizona took it out. In 1912, Arizona finally entered the Union as the forty-eighth state. Then they changed their consitution back to the way they wanted it.

Among the group of states between Canada and Mexico that all touch each other, Arizona was the last to gain statehood. More than a century and a quarter had passed since the

Union was formed. And many people living in the state right now remember what they were doing when statehood was announced.

Arizona's first governor, George W.P. Hunt, served seven terms—but not all in a row. And he set Arizona on the path it was to take into the present day.

One of the most important steps taken in those early days of

This photograph shows a modern irrigation canal under construction. The inset shows the gate of a canal. The gate is radio-controlled from a central location.

statehood was the building of dams. Starting with the Theodore Roosevelt Dam on the Salt River, these dams provided irrigation, electrical power, and water for new cities. The newest phoenix was rising strong and healthy on the Arizona desert.

As more land was irrigated, agriculture grew. The mines were putting out more copper. During the Great Depression of the 1930s, people all over the country left their homes looking for work. Many of them came to Arizona. During World War II, air bases were built in the state. And veterans who had been stationed here came back later with their families.

17

Above is the Morenci open-pit copper mine, the third largest in the world.

Arizona was clean, warm, and beautiful. When water and air conditioning were added, it seemed like paradise to a lot of people. The population rose by leaps and bounds.

But the people who had been here longest were not full participants in the new state. It was not until 1948 that Arizona Indians won the right to vote. In that year, the Supreme Court of Arizona ruled that the sections of the constitution that kept Indians from voting were illegal.

In the 1950s and 1960s Arizona began to change. Manufacturing became more important than agriculture in the state's economy. Tourists who came to enjoy the warm weather and beautiful scenery made tourism

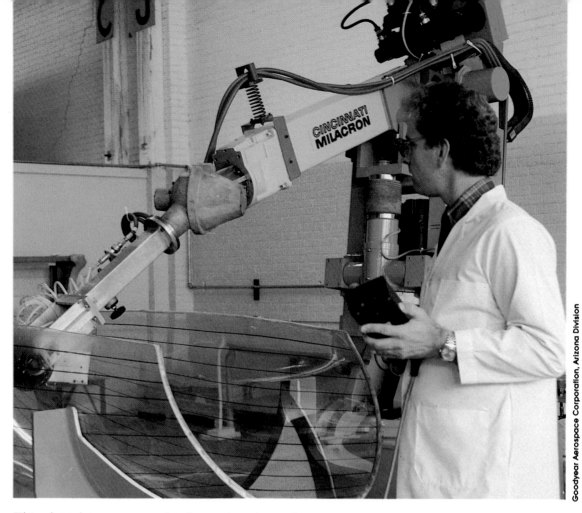

This robot is being programmed to do manufacturing work.

an important industry. And questions about the use of water began to arise.

Things began to change for the Indians of Arizona, too. Minerals were found on reservation land. Some of the tribes began to operate businesses. Navajo Community College opened in 1969. It was the first college ever built on a reservation.

And Arizona continues to grow. High-tech industries, looking for locations that will attract valuable employees, have chosen Arizona in droves. Today, about 75 percent of the population of the state lives in the two big metropolitan areas of Phoenix and Tucson.

The new history of Arizona is well on its way.

The Life and Near Death of a Town

"I came to Jerome in 1911. Jerome at that time, in appearance, was not greatly different from what it is now."

Jerome was a boom town. In the days of the rich copper mines, the population of Jerome was booming as fast as, maybe faster than, Phoenix is today. Herb Young remembers it.

"Living conditions were rather primitive. The streets were unpaved and crossing a street during rainy weather was quite an adventure. You'd be apt to lose your shoes. The town had twelve saloons. During the early days these saloons had entertainment. . . . But that was later banned."

It was not an easy life for the miners. If they played hard, they also worked hard. And the work was dangerous.

Phil Harris

"Quite a few men lost their lives in the mines in blasting accidents and falling ground. At one time there was a bad accident and a man got his leg crushed. They didn't have any medical facilities there. But this man who had been a doctor's aide in Louisiana borrowed some kitchen knives, amputated the leg and sewed it up. He took time off to go East and came back with some type of degree. But he was in Jerome for many years as a practicing physician."

In those days, Jerome was not a town of families and homes. The miners lived in hotel rooms for five dollars a month and ate in Chinese restaurants for five dollars a week, including lunches packed to take to the mines.

"Wages, at the time . . . well, they had different grades. There were the muckers, which were the common laborers down in the mine, got three and a half a day. The miners, the more experienced mining men who did the drilling, and the powder men got five dollars a day. They paid only once a month. That was because it interfered too much with the operations at the mine. The streets would be crowded on

At the far left is Herb Young against the background of Jerome. Above him is a photograph of a saloon in the Boyd Hotel at the time Jerome was a boom town.

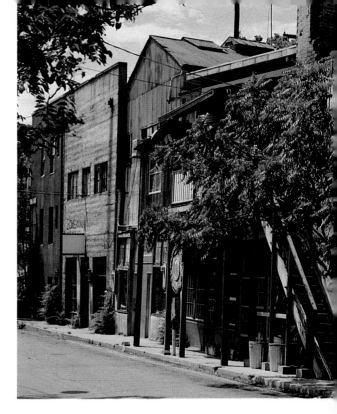

those days, just like you were giving the town a holiday. Marshals were kept busy. Many people didn't show up for work on the day after pay day."

The mines lasted until 1953. When the mines were worked out, the mining companies left. The population of Jerome fell from about 15,000 to about 115. Jerome was a ghost town.

Richard Martin came through Jerome years later. He was on a camping trip. But he liked what he saw and decided to stay.

"When I came here and when a lot of people came here, the town almost wasn't. . . . And we either jumped in to help get it together or the town would fall apart. Because there was nobody else. We became 'they.' Jerome came back to life because of the efforts of individual people doing sort of their own

things, and having it develop into something like the woodshop or like the various restaurants in town, because there was no business here."

Jerome isn't a ghost town anymore. There are about 400 people here, now. But will the people who brought it back to life be able to stay? Will Jerome's future include them?

"What people fear is that they're going to be moved out because their property is getting more valuable and their houses are becoming more expensive and there's chances for absentee landlords and things to make a lot of money. And so the future is going to be in how it grows."

22

Below is Richard Martin against the background of Hull Avenue in Jerome. At the far left is a photograph of the corner of First and Main streets as they looked in the early 1900s.

Copper, Cotton, and Computers

In many ways, Arizona is the state of tomorrow. During our brief history on earth, human beings have tended more and more to rule nature. Once, we were at its mercy. Then tools and simple engineering made it possible for us to work with nature. Now, to a greater and greater degree, nature is at our mercy.

The people of Arizona have gone into a desert, the kind of place that has not often supported human life in the past. And they have started from scratch.

Where there was no water, they have dammed rivers and brought water in. Where the heat was uncomfortable or even dangerous for people, they have put in air conditioning. Technology has made Arizona what it is. In return, Arizona

The Hoover Dam, on the Arizona-Nevada border.

Photos by Motorola

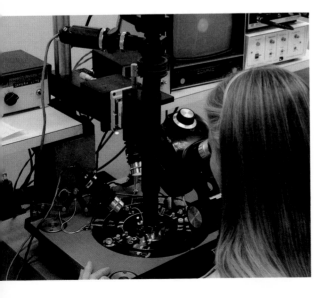

Present-day Arizona is one of the centers of "high tech" industries. The technician at the left is using an inspection instrument, and the one above is repairing a device.

has become one of the great homes of technology.

The industries we call "high tech" are unusual in the industrial age. They are, for the most part, clean. And they are not tied to a particular area because a particular natural resource is available there. What the high tech industries need more than anything else is people. They need people who are highly trained, with special skills.

And so the high tech industries choose locations that will be attractive to the people they need. Many of them have chosen Arizona.

For a long time, not many people wanted to or could live in Arizona. As a result, it remained clean and beautiful while other states were suffering from dirty air, water, and land. Today, clean is rare. And the beauty of Arizona has made it valuable.

The first, and so far the biggest, of the high tech companies to choose Arizona was Motorola. They moved into the state in the early 1950s. Now, they employ about 20,000 people, primarily in Phoenix.

Manufacturing of all kinds accounts for about 47 percent of the value of goods produced in Arizona. It employs about 15 percent of the people working in the state. The next two largest industries—mining and agricul-ture—together employ about 4 percent. The businesses that serve the needs of the people of the state make up most of the rest. About 7 percent are involved in construction, 25 percent in trade, 20 percent in government, and 22 percent in services. In other words, there are a lot of people employed in maintaining the lifestyle that attracts new industry and, of course, tourists.

The three major products manufactured in the state are nonelectric equipment, electric machinery and equipment, and transportation equipment. Technology.

Other manufacturing includes the processing of primary metals, food products, printed material, and stone, clay, and glass products.

Tourism is right up there with manufacturing in terms of the money it brings into the state. About $4 billion a year is brought into Arizona by tourists who come to swim in the south, ski in the north, and stand at the edge of the mighty Grand Canyon.

Mineral products are important to Arizona's economy, especially copper. Arizona copper mines produce about 60 percent of this country's supply of copper, about 10 percent of the world's supply. Other minerals are produced, too, but usually as by-products of the copper mining. About 32 percent of the value of goods produced in Arizona comes from mineral products.

About 20 percent of the goods produced in Arizona are agricultural products. And again, technology plays an important role.

Only about 3 percent of Arizona's land is used for crops. But the state's farmers use the most advanced methods of irrigation and cultivation. As a result, their production per acre is astounding. Cotton is a major crop. Because of the weather, vegetables and fruit can be grown in Arizona for almost the entire year. Arizona farmers supply winter fruits and vegetables to many colder, northern states. About 52 percent of the value of farm products in Arizona comes from crops.

The other 48 percent comes from livestock, mostly beef cat-

Arizona Office of Tourism

tle. Arizona has traditionally been ranching country because of the grazing land.

One thing to keep in mind when looking at Arizona is that only about 15 percent of the land is privately owned. The rest includes national and state parks, reservations, military bases. This is one of the reasons that so many people—one in five—are employed by the government.

Another important thing to remember is that Arizona has the third largest Indian popula-

Arizona Cotton Growers Association

The large photograph shows a sheep rancher in Monument Valley. The inset shows a cotton picker; cotton is one of Arizona's major crops.

tion in the country. There are over 160,000 Indians of various tribes now living in the state. Indian lands include an area as large as the state of West Virginia.

On Indian lands, life is still primarily agricultural. There are few businesses on the reservations. The treaties which guaranteed these lands for Arizona's Indians also guaranteed housing and education. Those promises have not always been kept.

There is a constant struggle on the reservations between honoring and preserving the traditional way of life and providing the necessities of life in the modern world.

If the water holds out, Arizona's economy will almost certainly continue to boom. If it doesn't, things could change in a big way. For all its high tech industries, the simple question of water remains the key to Arizona's future.

The rancher on the right-hand page is herding cattle. The woman at the right is frying bread. Below is Danny Lopez.

The Papagoes: Finding a Way Back

"Most of our songs are about nature—the mountains. We have names for all these mountains around here. We sing about the clouds, rain, different birds. . . . Because, according to our mythology, one of the most important things to the desert people would be the asking for rain."

The Papago Indians have been in southern Arizona for centuries. When the Spanish came, they were a peaceful farming tribe. They were gentle people who welcomed the strangers.

The Papagoes adopted their religion and much of their culture. As time passed, the Papagoes' own culture was almost lost. Today, children have to learn the Papago language in school.

Danny Lopez is a Papago who believes that relearning the old language and traditions is important.

"Every group of people . . . I read about them and I find out how they live, about their language. And it's important to them. I feel that, within my own people, the little ones should have some of that knowledge. It's just a part of us."

The desire of the Papagoes to save these parts of their past does not mean that they want to remain separate from the larger culture of their country. They believe that recovering their heritage will help them find their own special place in the world they live in. The children who know where they have come from will be stronger, prouder, and better able to decide where they want to go.

"I'd like to see our students someday become the doctors, the teachers, the lawyers, the professionals. And to work here on the reservation to help our people because we need that kind of help."

There is also much in the Papago culture that could help the whole state, Arizona, not simply the Indians themselves. Perhaps Danny Lopez and the Papago children will bring some of their love and respect for the mountains, the rain, and the water, back into our world.

Spanish Roots in Arizona Soil

"She was twelve years old when I first saw her at the ranch. . . . She was my sister's friend, but they went to California, and the years went by, and I saw her as a young woman, and she was seventeen, eighteen years old and I thought that was the time to catch the wife I'd been looking for. My family recommended her very highly so we got married and we are still married."

Enrique Aguierrie is a member of an old Spanish family in Arizona. He and his family live by their Spanish traditions *and* in the modern world. They have always been cattle ranchers. Today, they also farm, because it is necessary economically.

"Years ago, all we did was mostly cattle business, when my father was in his prime. We had a ranch where we had probably 18 to 20 thousand acres of land. They claim to have had about 8,000 head of cattle and many, many horses."

Mary and Rick Aguierrie, Enrique's children, carry on the ranching tradition. They have had to change some of the old customs in order to keep others. But they still keep the old values.

"Well, she's my daughter and she's helped me do everything we possibly can to keep what we have. But it seemed that, automatically, she was with me the most. At times we'd get her on the tractor and she'd do a man's work. We need more of this. My son, he took over,

Against the background of a windmill and Arizona cattle country are Enrique and Hjyino Aguierrie.

really. He's taking over and I think he's done a good job. We don't think alike in many things, but then again, I wouldn't expect him to agree with everything I say."

Things are very different now than they were in the days of the early Aguierries. There are women on tractors. There are trucks in the roundup instead of

The ranchers above are branding a calf. At the left are the Aguierrie brothers with the desert in the background.

horses. And some of the ideas Mary and Rick have for the future mean even bigger breaks with the past.

"We want to keep the cattle, I guess, maybe more than the farm operation. I love this place so much, with the sun and everything. We see a lot of winter visitors going by on the interstate, so we want to accommodate some of that and develop Red Rock itself as an adult-oriented resort. That would be able to accommodate some of the people that really love Arizona and have a cattle operation along with the rest."

But if Mary Aguierrie talks about resorts, it is only so that the Aguierries will be able to keep the cattle, keep that way of life alive. It is a way of life based on family and old Spanish values.

Hjyino Aguierrie, Enrique's brother, is an historian of Spanish cattle culture. To him, family is at the center of that culture.

"Well, I believe the Spanish tradition is a very beautiful tradition because the people are very close. . . . They're a little different from the Anglos. You know, the Anglo, generally speaking, when the boy gets to be twenty-one, 'All right,' they tell him, 'All right, boy, go make your own living.' In our family, I was forty and was still under my father's wing."

That part of life has not changed for the Aguierries. If they can manage it, it never will.

"I wish we could all keep on living together. That's what my folks expected of us . . . to stay together."

Cowboys, Indians, and Art

At the beginning of this century, the world was hungry for stories of the American West. In the streets of eastern cities, people bought thousands of cheap novels about strong, silent men who sat tall in their saddles and were quick with a gun. In the refined parlors of New York and St. Louis, they thumbed through magazine stories about shootouts and cattle rustlers and Indians, some noble and some savage.

The stories were often miles from the truth—and no wonder. Their authors were often miles from the West. But they caught the imaginations of people in London and Paris. And, until Al Capone and the other Chicago gangsters came onto the scene, those stories were the strongest image the

A painting by Frederic Remington.

37

world had of America.

One man, Zane Grey, stood out among the cowboy writers. He wrote so many books so quickly that the manuscripts were piled up on his desk when he died. New Zane Grey novels were being published for years after his death.

Zane Grey wrote about Arizona. His most famous books, including *Riders of the Purple Sage*, were set in this last outpost of the frontier.

Cowboy art, whether the novels of Zane Grey or the painting and sculpture of Charles Russell and Frederic Remington, has always been an important part of Arizona culture. Joe Beeler, a painter

now working in the thriving artist colony of Sedona, thinks he knows why.

"Cowboy art is a type of art that a great many people can relate to because it's realism. You don't have to have an art critic or a historian standing beside you, telling you what you should like. The average layman can look at a piece of western art,

At the left is Joe Beeler working on a piece of sculpture. Above is one of his paintings. It is called "Caught and Don't Know It."

Phoenix Art Museum, Cowboy Artists of America Exhibition, Joe Beeler

because it's realism, and enjoy it, or not enjoy it, on his own."

Cowboy art also brings alive a romantic past, filled with drama and excitement and a sense of danger. And that's one large part of Arizona culture.

But just as strong is the culture that was here centuries before the cowboy came. Mixed together as they often are, it's sometimes difficult to separate the two threads that make up that older culture—the Indian and the Spanish. Much of the Indian tradition is now filtered through the art forms brought in by the Spanish explorers and missionaries. But this art—pure or mixed—is very much alive in Arizona today.

It's there in the architecture of the cities. It's there in the weaving and the pottery. It's even there in what we have been calling "cowboy art."

And all of these cultural traditions use art to translate the beauty of the land itself. They take their colors from the tones of the earth. They draw inspiration from the grandeur of the sky.

Loving the Land

"Well, I'm just a kind of worn out newspaperman, really, but I was born over on the butte in eastern Arizona on a ranch. When I started working on the Republic, *all of this out here was just desert. There were no houses. And you can see the city has completely surrounded these mountains now."*

Ben Avery is an Arizona native. He is not part of the old Spanish culture or the Indian culture. He is part of the newest old group in the state. He is an old-time Anglo.

Born here before Arizona was a state, Ben Avery grew up with a respect for the land. Over the years, he has been part of the fight to preserve the natural beauty of his state. He walks in the desert and climbs the mountains. He writes about the land

and people that he loves.

At one time, Camelback, a mountain peak near Phoenix, was threatened by the city's development. But Ben Avery and others saved it.

"We started to try to acquire Camelback back when it became apparent that if the city didn't acquire it, if somebody didn't acquire it to preserve it, there was going to be houses all the way to the top and probably a neon-lighted restaurant sitting on top of it."

Thanks to people who care about Arizona, there are no neon lights on top of Camelback. They have also saved canyons threatened by irrigation dams and archaeological sites about to be buried under apartment buildings.

It seems that if you live in Arizona for any length of time, respect for the land simply grows in you. Or maybe the people who come to this state in the first place have something in them that responds to it.

" . . . I think everyone who came to Phoenix, and Arizona, came here because they love the country and the climate. And that is a spirit that kind of pervades our city. . . ."

Another Arizona native, Senator Barry Goldwater, puts it another way.

"Sometimes people say, 'Oh, we miss the pioneers.' Well, we don't because everyone who comes here is a pioneer. The young people! It's always been the young people who have made Arizona."

That's probably true . . . but you also have to include the young people like Ben Avery.

Ben Avery against a background of Camelback Peak.

The Future of the Phoenix

The future of Arizona depends on water. It's that simple and that complicated.

Life on the desert has always survived by using what water there is carefully and creatively. That's the secret of the cactus. That's the truth that the Indians and the Spanish understood. The question is how well the new Arizona will deal with it.

Each year, the state of Arizona uses about eight million acre-feet of water. An acre-foot is the amount of water that would cover an acre of land at a depth of one foot.

Right now, about one million acre-feet are used by the cities and factories. About seven million are used for agriculture. That water comes from the rivers and from under the

Phoenix is a symbol for the potential growth of all of Arizona.

earth. About two million come from underground.

In the future, more and more of the water that is now being used to irrigate the fields will probably go to the cities and factories. The question is how much and when.

Many people in Arizona feel that water is not being used properly. Part of the Arizona lifestyle includes swimming pools in the backyard and golf courses kept smooth and green. The city of Phoenix uses more water per capita than most major American cities. There are those who feel that this flies in the face of all that the past has taught us about the desert.

One of the major sources of water in Arizona is the Colorado River. But it is also a source for much of the Southwest, including southern California and the Los Angeles area. The Colorado River's water has been divided up by the federal government

The real key to Arizona's growth and future is water, most of which comes from the Colorado River (above).

into percentages. Arizona gets 19 percent, California 29 percent, and so on. But right now, the percentages add up to 110. The Colorado River is overbooked.

People in Arizona already talk about needing enough water for agriculture fifty years from now or a hundred years from now. They're looking at a time in the future when so much water will be used in the cities that there will be no irrigation for the fields.

Does the future of Arizona hold a colony of high tech industry and high living that depends for its food on the world outside? Will the new history of Arizona succeed where the Hohokams failed?

The future of Arizona is so bright that it dazzles the eyes. And yet, what is needed more than anything else is vision that comes from the wisdom of the past.

Important Historical Events in Arizona

1200 About this time, Oraibi is founded. It is the oldest community in the continental United States that is still being lived in.

1528 Cabeza de Vaca finds his way into Arizona after being shipwrecked off the Gulf of Mexico.

1539 The Franciscan priest Marcos de Niza, led by the black explorer Estevan, sees Zuñi Villages in Arizona, calls them golden cities, and claims the area for Spain.

1540 Another Spanish explorer, Francisco Vasquez de Coronado, goes as far into Arizona as the Zuñi River. A part of his group reaches the Grand Canyon.

1582 Silver is discovered near Prescott.

1692 Eusebio Kino, a Jesuit priest, founds the Guevavi Mission.

1751 The Pima and Papago Indians rebel against Spanish domination.

1752 The first Spanish fort is built near Tumac.

1776 Tucson becomes a fort.

1821 Mexico becomes independent of Spain, and Arizona therefore becomes part of Mexico.

1824 The Mexican government creates the Territory of New Mexico, which includes Arizona, and permits American traders to come into the territory.

1846 The United States is at war with Mexico. Tucson is captured by American forces.

1848 The treaty that ends the war with Mexico gives the United States all the area north of the Gila River. This includes a large part of Arizona.

1850 Congress creates the New Mexico Territory, which includes Arizona.

1853 The United States makes the Gadsden Purchase from Mexico and acquires the southern part of Arizona.

1857 Stagecoaches begin crossing Arizona.

1861- 1872 When the Civil War begins, the Confederacy claims Arizona. Cochise and other chiefs lead the Apaches against white settlers.

1863 The Arizona Territory is created by Congress with its capital at Fort Whipple.

1864 Arizona's capital is moved to Prescott.

1867 Tha capital moves again, this time to Tucson.

1869 The Grand Canyon is explored by a group led by John Wesley Powell.

1877 Arizona moves its capital yet again, back to Prescott.

1879 The Southern Pacific Railroad reaches Tucson.

1886 Indian fighting in Arizona ends when Geronimo surrenders.

1889 The capital moves for the last time, to Phoenix.

1911 Work is completed on the Theodore Roosevelt Dam.

1912 Arizona enters the Union as the 48th state. The capital is Phoenix, and the governor is George W.P. Hunt.

1929 The Coolidge Dam is completed.

1936 The Hoover Dam is completed.

1938 The Parker and Imperial dams are completed.

1939 The Bartlett Dam is completed.

1948 Arizona recognizes the right of Indian citizens to vote.

1963 The U.S. Supreme Court apportions water from the Colorado River to various states, including Arizona.

1965 Arizona becomes the first state with a woman chief justice of its state supreme court when Lorna Lockwood is appointed.

1971 London Bridge is moved from the Thames River in London to Lake Havasu City in Arizona.

1981 Sandra Day O'Connor, an Arizona judge, becomes the first woman appointed to the United States Supreme Court.

Arizona Almanac

Nickname. The Grand Canyon State.

Capital. Phoenix.

State Bird. Cactus Wren.

State Flower. Saguaro cactus.

State Tree. Paloverde.

State Motto. *Ditat Deus* (God Enriches).

State Song. Arizona.

State Abbreviations. Ariz. (traditional); AZ (postal).

Statehood. February 14, 1912, the 48th state.

Government. Congress: U.S. senators, 2; U.S. representatives, 5. **State Legislature:** senators, 30; representatives, 60. **Counties:** 15.

Area. 113,909 sq. mi. (295,023 sq. km.), 6th in size among the states.

Greatest Distances. north/south, 395 mi. (636 km.); east/west, 340 mi. (547 km.).

Elevation. Highest: Humphreys Peak, 12,633 feet (3,851 m). **Lowest:** 70 ft. (21 m).

Population. 1980 Census: 2,717,866 (53% increase over 1970), 29th among the states. **Density:** 24 persons per sq. mi. (9 persons per sq. km.). **Distribution:** 84% urban, 16% rural. **1970 Census:** 1,775,399.

Economy. Agriculture: beef cattle, cotton, milk, hay. **Manufacturing:** nonelectric machinery, electric machinery, transportation equipment, primary metals, food products, printed materials, stone, clay, glass products. **Mining:** copper, molybdenum, coal, sand and gravel.

Places to Visit

Grand Canyon National Park.
Apache Trail in Tonto National Forest.
Hopi Indian Villages in Navajo County.
Kitt Peak National Observatory, southwest of Tucson.
London Bridge at Lake Havasu City.
Meteor Crater in Coconino County.
Painted Desert.
San Xavier del Bac Mission, near Tucson.
Tombstone in Cochise County.

Annual Events

Arizona National Livestock Show in Phoenix (January).
Gold Rush Days in Wickenburg (February).
Cinco de Mayo Mexican Celebration in Nogales (May).
White Mountain All-Indian Pow Wow, Rodeo, and Dances on the Apache Reservation (June).
Frontier Days in Prescott (July).
Navajo Tribal Fair in Window Rock (September).
State Fair in Phoenix (November).

Arizona Counties

©American Map Corporation
License 18920

INDEX

MAR 5	DATE DUE	
D-5		
OCT 1		
OCT 10		
MAR 8